Can You See them Too?

Well! Can you?

Anne Germain

authorHOUSE®

AuthorHouse™ UK Ltd.
500 Avebury Boulevard
Central Milton Keynes, MK9 2BE
www.authorhouse.co.uk
Phone: 08001974150

First published by AuthorHouse 4/1/2011

ISBN: 978-1-4520-6643-1 (sc)
ISBN: 978-1-4520-6644-8 (e)

Introduction

The Greenough (pronounced Greeno) family is a family just like any other when you first meet them. There is a daddy, Norman, and a mummy, Jean, and three girls.

Susan, at six years old, is the oldest of them and very grown up. She was known for being a bit quiet and liking books. With her long wavy blonde hair and big blue eyes, she melted everyone's heart, especially Daddy's.

Anne, almost four years old was chatty and full of mischief. She had what most considered a very odd habit of always appearing to be talking to someone or of staring into space, and she had many 'invisible friends.' She had straight short strawberry blonde hair that was very fine and big blue eyes to match her sister's.

Sandra, the youngest at just eighteen months old was a little timid, but she was beginning to find out where she fit into the family, pushing her two older sisters as far as she could. Wherever she went, the pink and white rabbit called Bubbins was with her. The other two had teddies, but Sandra wanted Bubbins. She had wonderful auburn hair – very thick and long and curly – and a smile that would bring everyone running.

1

As the young family grew, their original home became too small and cramped, and it was agreed that it was time to move; so the Greenoughs went from a two-bedroom 1930's flat into a large rambling Victorian four-bedroom semi-detached three-story house on a main road. At the front of the houses was a mishmash of shops – from tiny old-fashioned sweet shops and a haberdashery to a modern bank.

The entrance to the new house was reached by walking down a long shaded corridor between the side of a bank and electrical shop to the right. To the eyes of a child, there was a magical garden awaiting exploration, as was the vastness of the old three-storied house. Its odd windows, each a different size, were black like an eagle's eyes, and they looked down on Anne from on high, blankly watching, just watching her.

Only Anne was aware of all those eyes watching her and her family; only she heard the chatter and murmurings.

Come and join the adventures of a mediumistic child; seen through her eyes, this story spans a few years in Anne's life beginning when she was a very young child and into her young adult hood. Feel what she felt, see how she saw, and watch her grow through life, constantly aware of others around her, watching, guiding, and helping.

Chapter 1

Moving Day

Hello. My name is Anne, and I'm nearly four!

I'm sitting in a big room just watching – watching people. Mummy and Daddy are putting stuff from Daddy's big lorry into the kitchen. They're going to show us around the new house and show me and my two sisters where we will be sleeping now.

Susan, my older sister, is already off looking into all the rooms of the big house. Sandra fell asleep on the chair ages ago; she's almost hidden under a pile of toys and her pink and white rabbit, Bubbins. She's been clinging to him since Mummy and Daddy said we were moving. She's only a baby. She's not even two. She isn't grown up like Susan and me. Susan is six and very grown up. Mummy say's we're both her little helpers now Sandra has arrived.

I've only ever lived in our little flat that we left this morning; Mummy said it wasn't big enough now Sandra had arrived, and so we had to move to a big house.

Daddy took us to see Nanny and Grandad Garbutt. They lived a long, long way away in the north, and it took days and days to get there. I think they had a little house. I've also been to Nanny and Grandad Greenough's. They live by the sea. Their house had lots of rooms and a great big red bell that rang when there was a fire to let Grandad know.

But I've never been anywhere as big as this house. There are three whole floors *full* of big rooms, with a garden and big buildings to hide in and a huge tree. Mummy said it's an apple tree, and we can have them for tea if they are eating apples.

I was happy at the flat and knew all the people who lived there with us. Only I don't think everyone else could see them all. No one else seemed to notice or hear them, so they were my secret friends to talk to and play with. I think Mummy knew I saw them and that they made me laugh and feel safe.

Here in this new house I feel very small; it has big rooms and high ceilings and new dark corners I didn't know yet for people who weren't there to hide and stairs, lots and lots of stairs going up and up and up all the way to the roof.

There are two children standing in the corner. They're wearing funny dark clothes – long skirts and stiff collars – not like my clothes bright and coloured and good to play in.

It doesn't matter today because Mummy said, 'If your clothes get a bit dirty today, it's okay. You can play in the new garden.' But I don't want to play in the garden.

I said 'hello' to the children, but they just looked at me and didn't say anything; they disappeared when I looked at them really hard. Mummy says not to stare at people because it's rude. So I didn't stare at them; I just look really, really hard to make them go.

I'm not frightened of the people I call 'No Bodies.' When I see them, they just make the room cold for awhile. That's what these two did just before they appeared. Sometimes they do talk to me. It's much more fun when they do. They have great stories and are fun to play with, and I can frighten my sisters. When I do that, I say to them, 'The Mr Nobody family's standing in the room watching us.' They get frightened and run and tell Mummy, which is funny.

Mummy and Daddy called for Susan to hurry up as they came from the kitchen into the big room. Mummy had beakers of juice and some jammy dodgers for us.

'Right, girls, time to have our picnic. Then we can all go and explore. When we get back, we can each draw a map, and then we'll know where everything is and not get lost in this big house,' said Mummy.

Chapter 2

Exploring the House

Mummy showed Susan and me some new little books and pencils for later, and we started out on our adventure from the kitchen. Daddy, carrying Sandra, led the way, and the rest of us followed. In the room after the kitchen was a big black hole.

'Mummy, what is that black hole meant to be?' I asked.

Mummy replied, 'A coal fire.'

Next to that stood a big white cupboard that went all the way up to the ceiling.

This was the room I'd been in earlier when I was watching the children. I looked round, and I could see they'd not come back.

Daddy said, 'We'll have this as the dining room. Do you think our big table will fit in here then girls?'

'Mummy, can we draw our maps straightaway?' asked Susan.

'Tell you what Mummy replied. 'How about I do a main map as we go along. Then you can both copy it when we get back from our adventure and I cook tea. That way, you'll be able to explore properly without having to worry about where to sit and draw. And you can add the people to the rooms when you know where we will all be sleeping,' Mummy replied.

Leaving the dining room meant going into a very long dark corridor. The underside of the stairs was on the right-hand side, and it was so cold here I could see my breath. I knew the No Bodies were watching us. I moved closer to Mummy as I looked for them. I knew they were there; I just couldn't see them yet.

Then I saw the lights! Lots of little sparkly lights moved around under the stairs, just as if they were walking beside us. It was them who were making the corridor cold.

I liked the lights. They bounced around before they appeared as people, making me laugh. The only problem was I walked into things and hurt myself watching them. Mummy calls me Dilly Daydream and tells everyone I'm away with the fairies. I did tell her that they're not fairies, but you know grown-ups don't understand these things.

The lights followed us as we made our way along to the next room. Our sofa and chairs from the flat were here, piled with boxes of toys waiting to be played with. There was another fireplace, but this time it had sticks and things in it ready to light, according to Mummy, so we had a nice cosy room to sit in.

Now we had the exciting bit of going up the first flight of stairs. The corridor was cold and very dark. There were no windows to let in any light. This was the kind of darkness that you can't explain – so dark you can almost touch it. The stairs, if possible, were even darker than the corridor. It was still so cold that you could see your breath. The light that Mummy had flicked on as she stepped on the first step did little to throw much more than shaky shadows on the walls, making it a scary place to be. And the whispering was starting.

I could hear the No Bodies getting louder becoming the whisper. I heard a whooshing in the background, faint like an out-of-tune radio playing lots of channels, all talking over each other:

'Hello.'

'Goodbye.'

'We're here. You see us. You hear us.'

'Come play with us.'

'What you doing?'

'Who are you? Anne, Jean, Mum, here.' Voices all merging together as one.

Daddy led the way, and we girls followed. We slowly climb to the first floor. At the top step, we could turn either right or left. Daddy turned to the left, leading us into a small dark hallway with an open door showing a big bright room that invited me in and a closed door to the right of the hallway. Our rocking horse was on the left opposite the closed door, hidden in the half light.

Heading into the bright room, we found ourselves in the biggest of bathrooms you can imagine. Daddy danced round with Sandra, pretending to be in a big ball room, there was so much space. This room was bright and warm, and the sun streamed in. Susan and I ran to look out the window. I could see out over the garden, which had a big bright green tree in the middle. There were buildings on the right and another garden on the left.

'Mummy, are there any children next door for me to play with when Susan is at school?' I asked.

'I don't know,' she replied, 'but we can have fun finding out when Susan is at school, can't we?'

'Right, now we have one of the most important rooms to find. You know the one. We've just passed it – the one that had the closed door. We passed it on our right as we come into the bathroom,' said Mummy.

Daddy stepped out of the bathroom and opened the door to reveal the toilet, a small cold narrow room with a tiny window up at the top. Appearing in front of me was a boy about eleven or twelve years old. He was tall and thin with messy curly dark hair like Daddy's, but Daddy's was very short. The boy's hair was longer.

Eyeing him, not sure whether or not he knew I could see him, I made my way into the little room with Daddy's encouragement. Then Daddy leant forward into the room and pulled the chain on the old toilet cistern, only to find it didn't work!

'Sneak up on it, and it will work,' said the boy.

I turned quickly and pulled the long chain like he said, and it worked!

We laughed over the sound of the rushing water, and the boy looked at me. 'You can see and hear me then?' he asked. 'My name is Kevin.'

I just nodded, turned, and ran to catch up with Mummy and Daddy, knowing that I had found a new friend in the house.

You reached the next big room by going up a little set of steps and the room being on the left this time it's the same side as the toilet.

As I caught up with everyone, Mummy was saying, 'This was the adult only sitting room.' The room was plain and square with a big fireplace that had a high mantle over it; I didn't see what the excitement was about. What was special about an adult sitting room? I was more interested in someone standing in front of the fireplace – a man with a big funny moustache and a jacket that came down the back of his legs and looked a bit like my pink dressing gown, only it was red and shiny.

The man with the funny jacket wasn't happy that Daddy was in his room. The man walked towards Daddy then straight through him. Daddy didn't even notice. It was so funny to watch when that happened.

The man looked right at me and said, 'I am master of this house. You have no right to be in my house.' Then he went away as quickly as he'd appeared. What an odd man.

The next room was going to be Mummy and Daddy's bedroom. This room was at the front of the house. Their bed, wardrobe, and cabinet were already in there, but like in every other room, there were boxes and boxes everywhere.

When I tried to look out of the window, I had to stretch on tiptoes to reach it. This room was even bigger than any of the others that we'd been in so far, with three big windows. It looked out over the flat roof of the building below. The roof looked like a big playground, but Daddy said we weren't to go out there because it wasn't safe. There wasn't really a way out that I could see anyway, but it was going to be fun looking.

This meant my bedroom must be right at the very top of the house, almost in the sky. The stairs leading to my room were much lighter. I could see a window at the landing, halfway between the first and second floors. With no curtains, the sun shone through with nothing to stop it.

As we got to the top of the next set of stairs, we looked out of the landing window, which was above the bathroom window but set back from it. I could see the slanting roof of the bathroom below. Then I could see for what seemed like miles and miles.

We went up the last six steps, and we reached the top of the world. Mummy said, 'This room is for Susan to have for her very own. She doesn't have to share anymore now that she's growing up.'

The room was smallish with a fireplace in front of you as you walked in the door and a window to its left that reached all the way down to the floor. Low, sloping ceilings made the room an odd shape, and a very big square box-like thing sat in the corner by the low window. Daddy said it was a water tank.

I looked round the room. I didn't feel anything cold at all, but I detected a light scent of pipe tobacco as I walked near the window. I saw no lights bouncing about at all. I had been amazed at what I could see from the window on the landing, but from this window I could see railway lines and miles and miles of roof tops.

The next room was the one I wanted to see – mine and Sandra's new bedroom. I ran from Susan's new room to my room. I stopped. The room was huge. Like Susan's school classroom, it was bright, long, and wide. Two big heavy wooden beds, a toy box, and ottomans that had been in Mummy and Daddy's room at the old house furnished the room.

Sitting on the ottoman was the young man I knew from the old house, he had always been part of my life the same as Mummy and Daddy were. He wore a smart navel uniform and held a big long cloth bag that looked like a sausage with one hand and the back of his head with the other. He seemed to always have a bad pain in his head when he came to see me; sometimes I knew he was there before I saw him because he gave me a pain in my head as well, and I could smell the sea.

Uncle Billy smiled, saying, 'Hello there, Anne. You didn't think I wouldn't come with you, did you?' Then he walked away towards the wall where the closed-in fireplace was and just went away.

Standing by the furthest bed that had Teddy on it was a pretty lady; her hair was up the same way that Mummy fixed hers, and she wore a long black skirt and white blouse with tiny little buttons from just under her chin all the way down to her belt, which her keys hung from.

I ran to my bed and grabbed Teddy in case she was planning on taking him. The No Bodies do that, you know – take things.

The woman said, 'Hello there. It's going to be nice to have children in the house again. The lady and master will be pleased too. They love children so.' Then she left as quickly as she'd arrived by just sort of fading away into the wall.

Susan and I ran round the room checking things out and looking from the single window, which looked at the trees and building across the road. That was difficult to do because, unlike Susan's window, which was low, this window was a much higher, like the one in Mummy and Daddy's room.

My room was at the front of the house right under the roof. It had high, sloping ceilings matching the lay of the roof outside. The sound of birds walking across the roof attracted my attention for a moment and I heard them cooing as they stood on the top of the chimney pots talking to each other.

I reluctantly left the room and went downstairs with Mummy and Daddy.

Daddy said, 'You and Sandra are in what I guess was the old servants' quarters when this house was first built. The bank that we walked past to get in here wasn't there when the house was built, but it was added many years after the house was first lived in by a well-to-do family.' He went on to say, 'The back of the house, where the kitchen and bathroom are, was added on at some time, and our dining room may have been the original kitchen and servants' room.'

As we walked down all the flights of stairs, I wondered whether the lady I'd met upstairs was one of the servants, but thinking hard, I was sure that this lady wasn't just any servant. She was too pretty and nicely dressed to be just a servant. I would have to ask Mummy about servants to find out exactly what they were.

Chapter 3

Two Very Different Maps

We decided to paint and not just draw the maps with the new pencils. Mummy was hanging up our maps to dry when she seemed to slow down and look at them. Mine, which was on the right, had lots of people in the rooms with colours all around them. Susan's on the left had the rooms, but they were empty. The only people were the family, which she'd painted at the side of the map.

I carried on painting, trying to get the colours to move the way they did around everyone I looked at. It wasn't easy. The brush was too big and clumpy, and when I looked at Susan to see her colours, they changed as she painted. Mummy's colours looked a bit damp. All across her chest area, her colour looked dirty. Normally, her chest was a lovely bright green, sort of sparkly like the stones in her broach. Now it looked like someone had tipped dirty water on her. It looked very funny, but it made me feel a bit uneasy, and I didn't know why.

I asked no one in particular, 'Why is it that, when you try and do a painting with water colours, they get so very wet all the time? It was making my colours all mingle into each other'.

Then Kevin, the boy who was hiding in the toilet, was standing next to me. So it must have seemed that, when I was complaining that my colours all went mushy, I'd been complaining to him.

Without moving, he tipped the jam jar of mucky paint water over, making an even bigger mess of my painting. The water dripped down the table onto the red stone floor. Upset, I cried out, 'Mummy, a Mr Nobody has spilt my painting water.' Oh dear, that was the wrong thing to say.

'Anne, if you spilt the water, just say you've spilt the water. It doesn't matter. Just don't tell lies and say that someone else has done it,' said Mummy in a stern voice, as she came into the dining room with a cloth to mop up the water.

Kevin stuck his tongue out at me and then just vanished, leaving only the cool chill in the air where he had been standing.

We'd been in the house most of the summer and none of the No Bodies I'd seen since moving in had bothered me very much. They were there and would sometimes just walk past, muttering to themselves, or in the case of Mummy and Daddy's sitting room, the man would push things off the mantel above the tall fireplace.

The only No Body I saw more than the others was the lady who I'd met in my room that first day. She used to come and tuck me in at night. She'd lived at the house since the master and lady had moved in; they had built the house a long, long time ago. I told Susan about the lady when went to bed, but she said I was just making her up.

Chapter 4

Spirits

I was sitting on the rocking horse holding his metal ears just rocking back and forth in the half light thinking. I felt the heat leaving the little landing area and knew that I had company. Without looking round, I said 'Kevin, I get upset when no one believes me about the No Bodies, but I've given up telling them. It's easier to just keep quiet – unless I want to frighten Susan and Sandra, that is. How come others can't see you?'

'I don't know,' he replied. 'I think that maybe some people don't open their eyes to see. I've been round Mummy and Daddy since I went straight into spirit instead of being born.'

'There are a few of us here that have grown up not being able to be seen by everyone,' he added.

'So you know Mummy and Daddy then?' I asked, slowly bringing the horse to a stop, my hands touching the cold metal of the horse below his ears, which had warmed up from the heat of my hands.

'Yes, I'm one of their children just like you.' Kevin allowed a little time for that to sink in before continuing 'There are three of us here that have been in spirit all the time – me and two brothers. We were meant to come into the family before you and your sisters, but it didn't work out.'

'Oh, so why didn't you get bodies like me, Susan, and Sandra then?' I asked Kevin. I was trying to work out why my brothers hadn't wanted to stay here and have bodies like me. Starting to slowly rock back and forth again, I waited for him to give me an answer.

'Sometimes things don't work out. I don't know why; they just don't,' he said. Then moving towards the stairs, he slowly became fainter and fainter until he was just gone.

I stayed rocking and thinking, talking to those voices that I could hear in my head, hoping that one of them would give me an answer that made sense. Not hearing anyone of them clearly enough, I tried something different.

'Uncle Billy, what did Kevin mean?' I asked, knowing that if I asked then I would get an answer from him.

I heard his voice clearly. 'Sometimes babies don't get born because things go wrong. They stop growing in their mummy's tummy, and they become spirits,' said Uncle Billy. 'What's a spirit then?' I asked him.

The reply came back to me, though I didn't see Uncle Billy. 'We're spirits, the people you call No Bodies. We don't need bodies anymore because we died and are spirits now. All those lights you see are spirits of people who have been in bodies before or of babies who weren't born. We can be anywhere and with anyone we want to be, but we often stay with our families.'

Just at that moment, Mummy's voice drifted up the stairs and brought my attention back. 'Teatime, Anne. Come down here now and stop playing,' Mummy called from what seemed very far away.

'Bye, Uncle Billy. I've got to go now,' I said to the air.

I just heard his laughter in the distance in reply.

Chapter 5

Halloween

I was walking on one side of the pram, and Susan on the other; we were going to school. Mummy was talking to Sandra, who was wrapped up against the chill in the air and the light frost. All sorts of things hung from the top of the big window of Jarman's, one of the sweet shops; there were big black spiders and cobwebs, witches, ghosts, and a big broom stick.

Susan asked, 'Mummy, what are all those in the window for?'

Mummy said, 'It's Halloween at the end of the week, the day when all the ghosts and spirits were meant to go out and haunt. It's the old celebration of the start of winter and All Hallow's Eve. When you get home from school tonight, I'll tell you all about it, but for now, hurry up. We'll never get you to school at this rate.'

Hurrying the last bit to school, Susan and I ran along the grass until we got to the gates. Susan ran on ahead into the school, just as the bell rang. I started to follow her through the gates.

Mummy caught us up. Catching me by the arm, she said 'Oh no you don't, young lady; you're not old enough yet to join Susan. Next year, you will go.'

Mummy got Susan settled in class. Then we started the walk back home. Well, Mummy walked. I hitched a lift on the pram with Sandra. There was just enough room for me to squeeze in beside her under the blankets.

As we made our way past the big old houses, I looked out from round the side of the pram into the top window of the first house past the grass by the school. The little girl who normally looked out of the window was standing there, her long blonde hair in ringlets like Mummy did Susan's sometimes. I wished my hair was long enough to put in curls like Susan's, but Mummy said it was too fine to do that with and it was better kept short. I waved at the little girl as we went past, and she waved back, her curls bobbing up and down like little corkscrews.

'Right, you two, just time for us to do a bit of shopping before getting back home. Then we'll lay the fire in the sitting room, and I can do the ironing,' Mummy said to Sandra and me.

'Mummy, can I do some paintings?' I asked quietly as we rolled along, Sandra having been lulled asleep by the motion of the pram.

'If you want to,' Mum replied. 'Or you can come and keep me company while I do the ironing and I'll tell you some stories.'

I didn't get to reply because it wasn't long before the warmth and motion of the pram had also lulled me into the same sleep it had sent Sandra into. My sleep was dotted with visits from my spirits friends.

Mummy, true to her word, explained all about Halloween when Susan came home from school. It all seemed silly to me. Why be afraid of those who have died? They seemed nice enough to me most of the time, although I wasn't sure about the ugly faces on the monster masks for sale in the big sweet shop.

Mummy said that it was a way of saying goodbye to people who had died and old scary things but also of remembering all the people you knew who had died and gone to heaven like Jesus.

We'd learnt about Jesus from Mummy, and she said that, when I was bigger, I could go to the school on a Sunday at the church. We walked past the church on the way to the park, but I wanted to go to the church near the big shop called Fred's Emporium. Fred's had lots and lots of things, and the shop was full of No Bodies, who were often around old things as they didn't want their things to be given away.

I don't think they know they are spirits sometimes because of the way they talk and move around; they walk round tables and not just through them like normal No Bodies. Often I couldn't tell the difference between the normal people and the No Bodies.

One day, I asked if I could go to the other church. Mummy said it wasn't for children, but I felt as if I belonged there, and I didn't know why. A lot of bright No Bodies with lovely white lights glowing inside them were there; they all looked happy and smiley all the time.

I thought that I should go to that church – the one Mummy said was called Walton Spiritualist Church – and not the other one. I was too little to have a say in which church I went to, but I felt that, one day, I would be able to go inside and find the No Bodies who were so bright and had lovely lights inside them.

Chapter 6

Time Flies

Susan hated the man on the stairs; he hid in the shadows just out of the way and made the stairs really cold. I saw him when I came down one night. I couldn't sleep. I was looking for Mummy, and he blocked my way. He never fully showed himself. He was a shadow – a thick black shadow. I wasn't scared of him, but he wasn't nice. He was a bit silly really. He didn't like children, especially children like me. He whispered, 'freak child,' when I walked past him. I wondered what a freak child was.

I wasn't sure if Susan could see him, but I knew she could feel him because he made her shudder when she walked through him. He would get quite cross when we'd do that; he seemed to think that we should all be able to see him. I didn't think he knew he was a spirit yet, like the No Bodies in the shop. Maybe some grown-up should tell him, and maybe he or she could tell the others at the same time.

Mummy's colours still weren't right; the darkness across her chest was getting darker. It had gone from being a damp brown colour to almost black. It wasn't right; I knew it wasn't right.

Mummy and Daddy had been talking quietly together a lot. Daddy looked very worried and sad, and Mummy cried. Our cousin, Gordon, and his wife, Margaret, came round from where they lived and talked to Mummy and Daddy in hushed tones as well. I liked Margaret and Gordon; she was very pretty, and he made us laugh. Gordon was Aunty Mary's son, which was what Mummy said made him our cousin. Aunty Mary lived next to Nanny and Grandad by the seaside.

Mummy said that Margaret was coming to look after us for a while because she had to go to hospital, as she wasn't well and needed an operation to help make her better.

They all look very worried, so I worried. Susan was very quiet, so I thought she was also worried. We just looked at each other. Sandra was too little to worry about things that were going on; the only thing was she had become very clingy to Mummy and cried when she couldn't see her.

It was all dark, and I was meant to be asleep. Mummy was not going to be here tomorrow because Daddy was taking her to hospital. I'd been calling Uncle Billy in my head for a long time, and he didn't seem to be coming to talk to me.

I kept asking and asking, and then a light, which came from near the chimney, started to creep into the room; it was a beautiful light – all sort of shimmery blue and white. The room felt warm, and it was very quiet. I could see a lady starting to take shape like a real person. She didn't look like a No Body. She is more like us. She came close to my bed and didn't actually walk; she just sort of glided there.

She said she was a Healing Angel and belonged to Mummy and that I wasn't to worry about Mummy anymore – that although she would be away from home for a little while, she would be coming home because she had a lot of work to do here on the earth and it wasn't time for her to be a spirit yet. I didn't remember the lady leaving; all I remembered was feeling her touching my face, and it felt so good – gentle and warm. I think I must have fallen asleep. The next thing I knew, it was morning, and Mummy was coming and giving us all a kiss, saying goodbye, and telling us she loved us all.

Mummy seemed to have been gone for ages when Daddy said he was going to take us to see her. He told us that we were going to have to see her through a window because children weren't allowed in the hospital. The hospital was a long way away from home, and it took awhile for Daddy to drive us there in his car.

We had to walk up a big long hill when we got there and sit outside of a long building and a big grassy bank. Daddy said he was going to go inside and stand by the window near Mummy. We waited for ages, and then I could see Daddy waving at us. Then he opened the window and called our names. Nurses stood next to him holding a big mirror.

When I looked in the mirror I could see Mummy; she looked very little in her big bed. She tried to wave but didn't seem able to move her arm very well. Daddy passed messages to us through the window letting us know what Mummy was saying. Sandra started to cry, and Margaret had to take her for a walk because Mummy started to cry to.

After awhile, the nurse told Daddy that Mummy needed to be quiet, and we all had to leave. I didn't want to leave, but then I saw the lovely lady who had visited me standing next to Mummy. Mummy's angel was smiling at me. I knew Mummy was coming home soon; the lovely lady was looking after her.

Mummy came home a little while later, but she was tired all the time and cried a lot. She said that she'd had two operations, and because of the second operation, she wasn't going to be able to have any more babies. Mummy and Daddy talked about her having had cancer. They hoped that the two operations had taken it all away, but she would have to keep going to the hospital to be checked out.

I looked at Mummy's colours. They were all bright again, with no darkness no damp colour. There were fuzzy areas, but they looked bright. And I thought, because of the way Mummy held herself, that maybe they were the areas that the operations were on.

Mummy was home; Margaret and Gordon could go home now. I loved them lots, but Margaret wasn't Mummy, and she wasn't as much fun when she told us what to do as when she just visited us for tea.

It seemed like a long time since we'd moved into our home; summer and Christmas went by quite quickly really.

The year after we moved here, I joined Susan at her school. I had been so excited to start, but it wasn't as much fun as Susan and Mummy said it would be. The No Bodies were there, and they didn't let me listen to Miss; she was my teacher.

I was always in trouble for not listening, but I managed to work out a way of reading without reading; the No Bodies told me what was on the page, because all I could see were lots of squiggles and mixed up shapes that kept moving on the page. Then when I was asked by Miss what something meant, I could answer, and no one bothered me.

Only problem I encountered was spelling tests. Miss kept giving silly spelling tests, and those I couldn't do. Watching the angels in the sky, flying in the clouds or looking at all the lovely colours that surrounded everyone in the school was much more fun.

Mummy came to the school today because Miss had upset me. She'd told me I was thick and didn't learn things properly; I was being taken out of the normal class and put into a room with some others to have 'special' reading lessons. I really don't know why she was bothering! What was the point of reading when I could ask the No Bodies to tell me what was on the page and then just remember the words?

I'd heard one of the teachers say, 'Don't worry about Anne. She'll never need to work. She will just leave school, marry, and have babies of her own.'

Sometimes I thought grown-ups thought I wasn't clever! But the No Bodies told me I was very clever because not everyone else can see them or speak with them when they wanted to.

I always tried to find something else to do at the playtimes; playtimes were horrible; other kids from all different classes were nasty because of what I could see. They told me I was a freak! 'Freak! Freak! Freak!'

They'd catch me in the toilets and put soap in my eyes, saying, 'What can you see now, freaky?' They'd bang loud noises near my ears and shout. 'Who you talking to, freaky?' I hated it when they hit my head; it was like being hurt inside all the time. The top of my head always hurt. I didn't like anyone touching my head; I didn't want anyone touching my head ever!

I wasn't mad, and I wasn't a freak. I was Anne.

I hated school! But I didn't hate it as much as David did. He wouldn't come into the school unless I held his hand. He didn't see the No Bodies like me. He was just a little different from the other boys; he was more like me and my sisters I think. He liked our toys and dolls and prams and playing gentle things. His daddy and my daddy worked together. They both drove the most enormous lorries full of meat you'd ever seen.

Daddy came home from work recently and had a little dog with him. Mummy said that the dog couldn't stay because she didn't need another thing to look after. The dog was a little girl dog, and her name was Julie. Daddy said she was a terrier, and that made her a ratter. He said she would go down holes and look for rats.

I wondered why Daddy had brought her home, but he said that she didn't have a home, and we were going to look after her till he found her a new home. I wanted to keep her for always. Maybe Daddy could take her and me out in his lorry at the same time.

Spending time in Daddy's lorry was fun; he would wake me up early in the summer holidays and let me go with him on his deliveries. If I was really lucky, his delivery would take him down to Nanny and Grandad's village, and I would get to have a cup of tea and see Nanny with her dog in the garden. Sometimes, we even got to see the sea if Daddy was ahead of his schedule.

Then when we were there and early I got to spend time with Great-granny Greenough, Daddy's Nanny if the weather was too bad to go to the sea. She must be a hundred years old. She was so old, she couldn't walk about. She was teaching me to play a card game called patience. I liked talking with her. She told me stories I understood because some of them were about people I had seen – No Bodies who visited Daddy at our home, only Daddy didn't see them.

I had a new friend at school called Katie she started school later than me. Katie didn't call me a freak. She saw No Bodies too. We had fun and got to play lots without the others bothering us. I didn't think that Katie would see No Bodies forever. Kevin said it wasn't normal for children to see them for long – something to do with being told that the No Bodies were only a figment of their imagination and it being easier for them not to tell anyone what they saw.

It was soon going to be time to move up to the bigger school where Susan had gone. I was sure that the kids would not be as nasty there.

I didn't know what to do – Katie's dad was moving her family away. Who was going to be my friend now? Katie would be going to some place called South Africa. I looked on the map, and it was miles and miles away. She would miss our Christmas party, which Daddy was going to take us to. I wouldn't have anyone who understood the No Bodies anymore; I would be back to being the freak. I cried so hard I couldn't sleep, and when I came down and told Mum that I didn't want Katie to leave, she said that we could write to each other and be pen friends.

It just wasn't the same! I still couldn't write properly. It was hard when all the letters moved and were oddly shaped and didn't make any sense to me.

Mummy said that we could keep Julie because she was good with children. Daddy took her for a walk every night before he went to bed. She was lovely and liked to be dressed up in my dolls' clothes and sit in my dolly's pram.

I had seen a new No Body in the house it is Grandad; the Grandad from the long way away in the north had come to visit me. I hadn't seen him for awhile, not since we went up to see him in the house where he lived with Nanny. He said that Nanny was coming to live with us at our house soon.

I wondered where she'd sleep. There was plenty of room for a bed in mine and Sandra's room, but I didn't think she'd want to share with me and Sandra, and Susan wouldn't want to share her nice little room.

I soon found out where Nanny would stay. Mummy was losing her lounge. I hadn't thought that would happen. I wondered what that nasty man would think when he found out Nanny had his room.

Chapter 7

The Visit

We had so much excitement in the house today. Mum and Dad had been busy getting extra beds sorted out and making room. Some of Mum's family was coming to stay. We'd been up to visit them in the north, but they were coming down here today.

Aunty Nancy gave me a necklace to keep when we visited her way up north because Susan went out somewhere special with Debbie, and I had to stay behind with Sandra and Mum, which wasn't what I wanted to do.

When I got home, I buried my necklace as special treasure in the garden to keep forever, like in the story books Mum had been reading to us, only I couldn't quite remember where I buried it. I thought it was by the clothes line post, but when I went to dig it up again, all I found was some string. I wondered if the fairies that were in the garden took it.

I was so excited that Aunty Nancy and my cousins, John, Debbie, and Bruce, were coming for Christmas; I hadn't seen them for ages and ages. Nanny was very excited about them coming down because she hadn't seen them for a long time. Bruce was nearly my age, Debbie was Susan's age, and John was very grown up.

We would meet them at the station. It was a long way to come by train, Mum said. Driving was easier, but Aunty Nancy, like Mum, didn't drive. Dad said they all drove him mad, but Mum threw the kitchen towel at him when he said that.

Bruce was really good. He didn't mind my No Bodies at all. He thought it was funny when I told him they were there. Debbie talked more to Susan than to me, so I told Bruce all about Great-granny Greenough. She used to sit in the big chair down at Nanny and Grandad's, but now she came and visited us; I wasn't sure, but I thought she must have died now. I thought she was hundreds of years old. I still played the game she taught me to play called patience.

Bruce and I made everyone laugh by dressing up and pushing a pram round my bedroom pretending to be Great-granny Greenough and wearing big bloomers. It wasn't easy trying to make big baggy knickers out of my pyjama bottoms, but we managed it.

I asked her if she minded us playing like that, and she said she didn't because I had liked sitting with her when she was like us. She had good stories to tell me, and they were often about the No Bodies that I could see in the house down at Nanny's and the ones that visited Daddy.

Uncle Sonny, my dad's brother, said he's been in spirit for a long time. There is a picture on the wall that he says is his cross; the picture is very old with a little photograph of Uncle Sonny on the top left hand side it's an old army picture and in the centre a slightly larger faded black and white photo of a grave cross. Nanny always has a poppy flower near it; it makes her sad when she looks at it.

We were all going out to the park today to give Aunty Nancy some quiet. She needed to sleep because she hadn't been well.

We had all woken Aunt Nancy up really early for Christmas Day, and she'd tried to light her cigarette the wrong way round. Mum and Dad thought it was so funny as we sat round the fire, which was still lit from the night before.

In the park, there was a paddling pool, but it was too cold to use it – we would have to break the ice so it's a good job the man in the park would drain it at the end of the summer. We could play in the pool, running round and round, without getting wet.

I wanted to get out of the house today. There were lots of people whispering – both those who were No Bodies and Mummy and Aunty Nancy. Aunty Nancy had the same nasty colours that Mummy had had before she was in hospital; only with Aunty Nancy, the colour was almost everywhere. So I thought that either she hadn't been in hospital long enough or her angel hadn't visited her yet to make her better.

No, I didn't think Aunty Nancy was well at all. Her colours normally were bright and cheerful. Now, they seemed to be getting very distant from her as well as being dark, like they weren't attached to her anymore.

She had the same funny smell that Mum had when she had gone into hospital a long time ago. Mum's colours had never gone distant and looked as if they weren't attached to her anymore. I needed to ask the No Bodies what was happening. I didn't like the whispering when I saw things that didn't look right.

The No Bodies whispered to me when I was standing in the kitchen helping Mummy. They said it was a time of change and that I just needed to be a good girl for Mum at the moment because there was going to be a new person joining spirits.

Our holiday was over all too fast; Aunty Nancy and the cousins went home and the house was very empty. Nanny was very quiet today, and Mum was crying when I walked into the room after school. But when she saw me, she turned away very quickly. I thought that my aunty was going to become a No Body and come to visit us all the time soon. I thought that is what the No Bodies had meant when they'd said a time of change was coming and a new person would join the spirits.

It didn't seem like anytime at all before Mum had a phone call after which she went up north and spent some time looking after John, Debbie, and Bruce because Aunty Nancy needed to go into hospital again.

Nanny stayed with us to care for us. She'd have tea ready for us when we got in from school.

Mum had been away for a little while, and she'd ring Dad most nights to speak and to say good night to us kids. I was sitting waiting for Mum to call when I noticed Aunty Nancy standing next to Nanny giving her a gentle kiss on the top of Nanny's head before she just faded away as quickly as she'd appeared.

About an hour later, we were all in the dining room after having finished tea when the phone rang. Dad answered it and was very quiet. He then turned to us and said that Aunty Nancy had gone to join Grandad and passed away into spirit.

That night, posh Aunty Mary from London came to collect us to take us to stay at her house while Dad took Nanny up to see Mum. The funeral had been organised, and the adults need to be there for John, Debbie, and Bruce.

I didn't know who my cousins were going to live with now. They hadn't lived with their dad, just their mum, so I wondered if they would come back with Mum, Dad, and Nanny.

Later I found out that they went to live with their dad, and I didn't get to have my Bruce come and live with me after all.

Chapter 8

New School

I would be moving into the middle school today. My new school was at the same location as my old school, so I didn't know why it was called 'middle school'; maybe it was because the new school was held in the middle building.

Nearly all the same people were moving up with me. My teacher said that we were going to be in different classes. I was going to have a new teacher called Mr Brand. I wondered if he would think I was a freak.

Well, it's only been a few weeks of going to the new school and I know that Mr Brand didn't seem to think I'm a freak, so I guess that was one bonus. However, he told me to tell Mum that my eyes needed testing! And that was just because I asked to move from the back of the class to the front because the words on the board were all smudgy. Looking at the board was a bit like when the No Bodies were around; then they were clear and everything else was smudgy.

Maybe I should just have carried on as I had before, listening to the No Bodies and writing what they said to write. But when I did that, I only got into trouble, so

I guessed being told I needed to get my 'eyes sorted out' was better than that.

One day, I was doing an art lesson, and I decided to paint the No Body lady who stood next to me nearly all the time. She was lovely, so calm and gentle. She wore funny clothes like my godmother Margaret's best friend. Margaret told me her friend was a nun. She came to visit us one evening in the summer ages ago. I really liked her because the colours all around her were whites, purples, blues, and greens, which told me that she was a very special lady and had time for everyone.

I didn't think Margaret's friend would continue wearing these clothes because Kevin told me that she'd walk a different pathway in the future. I didn't have a clue what he meant. I'd like to work like she does. Maybe I could become a nun.

When I got up this morning, Mum said that our dog, Julie, had decided to take herself for her evening walk on her own last night because Dad was late home from work. She said that Julie had gone out on her own and when she'd come home and climbed into her bed, she was very ill. Mum said Julie had been hit by a car and wasn't well enough to stay here with us; she needed to go to Jesus.

It took me a long time to understand what Mum meant because Julie had been on my bed as normal when I got up. She wasn't meant to come all the way up the stairs, but she used to do it when we got up in the mornings, like she was checking to see if we were all awake.

I didn't see her come down the stairs. She was just sitting under the table like normal, wagging the little bit of tail she had left. I didn't want to go to school now because I knew when I came home, Julie wouldn't be there as normal. Now I would only see her with the No Bodies, and she wouldn't be warm to hug and wouldn't try to eat the tablets Mum took to settle her tummy.

Susan and Sandra cried about Julie being with Jesus, but it didn't make sense to cry; she was still here with us.

Not long after Julie became a spirit we were going on a trip out of school; we were going to Hampton Court Palace. I knew it wasn't far away because we passed it on the bus when we went to Kingston to go shopping with Mum. It was going to be fun; we were taking a packed lunch and drink and everything. Mum was giving me some money to spend in the shop when we had finished.

The coach pulled in by the side of the road outside the palace; we all bundled off and went in a long crocodile to the entrance. Everywhere inside I saw No Bodies wearing some very odd clothes! The rooms made me feel very odd, like I was floating round and round. I didn't like the feeling; it was as if I was travelling in time, going backwards and falling out of my body. It took all my energy to stop myself from falling as I listened to the people, who wanted my body for themselves so that they wouldn't be No Bodies anymore.

I didn't like a lot of the rooms. They were empty in one way but very busy with No Bodies pulling me this way and that way at the same time. The No bodies smelled really bad, and their clothes were heavy and dirty and made of really thick material with beads and things. The dresses of the ladies dragged on the ground and were tatty as well as dirty. We went into the big kitchens and all I could see was a boy standing by a fire turning a big handle. A big pig hung over the fire cooking; it smelled lovely, but the boy was dirty and didn't have shoes on or anything.

He looked round at me and sort of looked through me. He was a different sort of No Body; it was if he could see me but at the same time couldn't see me! There are a few here like that; they just seemed to keep doing the same thing over and over. I didn't like them. They made my skin go all crawly and funny.

There were some scary No Bodies here too; they were all scabby, and their faces were purple and blotchy. They were not nice.

I wanted to go home. I didn't like learning history in palaces like this; it was scaring me, and No Bodies didn't normally scare me.

I went on lots of other trips with school to all sorts of places. Some were as nasty as the first, and others were nice. But I still didn't like old buildings. They crept into my skin and made me feel wrong, like the No Bodies were trying to take my body for themselves.

And the school bullies continued to bully me. I was frightened of a girl called Frances who was in Susan's year. Every time I went into the playground, she called me nasty names and pushed me around. What was the point of telling anyone? No one believed me when I told them about the No Bodies, so why would anyone believe me about her?! This school was no better than the last. I wished I didn't have to go to school, but Dad said I had to.

At last it was time to go on our summer holidays, so there would be no more bullying for a long time. When we come back, I was going to change class. My new teacher would be Mr Titherly; he was an art teacher. I liked being able to paint and draw. I'd like to design things like clothes or make nice pictures for people to hang on the wall when I grew up. Mum said I couldn't be a nun because I was a member of the wrong religion. I didn't see why that should stop me, but she said it would.

I didn't have problems in art because I didn't have to write things. I was always in trouble for not spelling things correctly. I just didn't understand why the letters never stayed still on the page; they are all the wrong way round. How was I meant to know the difference between a *d* and a *b* when they never stayed in the same place?

In art I could make things – from enamel a little ring and pendants, from wood a lamp base and box for my rings and pottery a dinosaur. I could lose myself and just talk with the No Bodies. People just thought I was concentrating; they didn't know about my conversations, and I didn't want to tell them. It was my world, not theirs.

Chapter 9

Long Hot Summers

It was still dark when Dad came and woke me up. He said it was 4.00 a.m., and nothing was awake yet. He gave me some breakfast and a cup of tea, and then we climbed into his car. He'd put all the fishing tackle into the boot last night. We had sandwiches that Mum made and a flask of hot tea for us to take this morning.

I loved fishing with Dad. It was so silent as we'd just sit and I'd watch the water lights bounce up in all colours, as the ripples made their way from fish moving under the surface. Birds dove down and caught the flies as they glided close to the surface.

But now we were in the car driving to a place Dad calls Black Boys' Reservoir. We had to park the car up and walk across some fields to get to where we were going to fish today.

A strange orange light filled the sky. Dad said his old saying that he said when he meant that the weather wasn't going to be good – 'Red sky at night, shepherds' delight; red sky in morning, shepherds warning.' That was silly because the sky was orange today!

We got near the water, and Dad found me a really nice spot where I could sit and have all the bits I needed for fishing close by – shade because I burnt too easily (Mum made Dad promise to keep me out of the sun for at least some of the day.), a spot to put my gear, and close enough to the water to put my fish into my keepnet.

Dad had gotten me all my own fishing stuff. I had fishing rods; reels; and a box that he'd made for me and painted pale green to put all my hooks, lines, and floats in. I had tools for getting the hooks out and little lead weights to put on the lines and a dark green round box with all my own maggots in it. I even had a big green umbrella and net to bring my fish in with if they were really big; I normally just caught Anne-sized fish according to Dad. He said he got the big fish.

Sometimes we didn't catch anything, but it didn't matter. Dad was going to take me sea fishing when I was bigger, out in a boat like the ones we'd seen when we'd gone to Nanny and Grandad's.

Here by the water, I could just sit and talk with the No Bodies. It was quiet, and they didn't have to shout all at the same time like they normally did. They said it was because there was less to distract me. Talking quieter than normal, they told me stories and things about who they were and where they came from.

I liked some of the No Bodies, I had some new No Bodies now that were with me; they said they were there as teachers and helpers for me in my life.

One man was always with me, no matter where I was or who I was with. He made himself appear as a little man who sat on my shoulder. To make me laugh, he liked to change his colours so I would never know quite what he was going to look like. I loved it when he came as a little green man with purple spots. I told my sister Susan about him when we walked to school. He told me he was there to protect me and, when I was older, he'd show me how he'd really looked when he was in his body a long, long time ago.

I had a new No Body friend called Jimmy. He was always covered in black soot and wearing no shoes and tatty trousers when he came to see me. He said he was a sweeps boy and that he'd gone up a chimney but that he'd grown too big and gotten stuck. His sweep thought he was trying to run away and lit a fire under him to make him go up. He said he just couldn't breathe anymore and found he was free when the lady made of light came close to him.

He told me all about this beautiful lady with the wings. He said she was all lit up like she had hundreds of candles burning inside her. He said she told him she was an angel collecting lost boys, and he felt happier than he ever had felt before. I told him his angel sounded like the lady who had looked after my mum when she was ill. He thought maybe we were talking about two different angels, as the one who had come for him was special and spent all her time collecting lost people.

After Jimmy met the lady, he was able to look back and see himself as he had been, just as he showed himself to me. He showed me how he'd been stuck in a big bend in the chimney in a big house near Brighton. I told him I'd been to Brighton, or it could have been Littlehampton, with Mum and Dad to see a very special film called *Bambi* but it had made me cry because I was sad when Bambi found out his Mummy had been shot.

Jimmy said that Bambi's Mummy must have been collected by the angel because that was her job. I liked the idea that lost people were collected. Jimmy said that we were always collected when we didn't need to have a body anymore – that we were never left on our own. We often talked about dying and what it really meant. Jimmy said that it was adults who were frightened of going but not children because children remembered where they'd come from.

Before I knew the time, Dad was saying it was time for us to go home. I packed all my bits away and let my fish go. It wasn't right to keep them; if we let them go, they would grow into big fish one day.

We got home to find that Uncle Bob, Mum's baby brother, was there. I didn't know why they said baby; he was as tall as the house! Uncle Bob had come to take us out to the pictures and then have lunch in Walton Wimpy. He played guitar and painted pictures; he seemed so very sad, even though he laughed a lot of the time. He worked in the lollipop stick factory, and he brought sticks for us to make houses and things for our dolls out of. He worked the night shift and slept during the day.

Uncle Bob had daughters up in Hartlepool where Mum and he grew up. Wendy and Julie came down once with

Aunty Agnes, but Mum wasn't happy because they had bugs in their hair from school, and Mum had to treat us all, even them. Susan and Sandra didn't like it with their thick long hair. Mine was short, so the treatment was quick.

I asked Mum if we'd have had to treat Julie if we still had her, but Mum said fur wasn't quite the same as hair. I don't see the difference myself; fur was just shorter.

Uncle Bob sometimes comes round with Uncle Frank, who helped Dad garden. Sometimes Uncle Frank had dinner with us. He was another uncle who looked sad; his eyes never smiled.

Mum said that summer was always a busy time. We normally went and stayed with Nanny and Grandad. But this year, we were going on a long journey to the Isle of White, and Uncle Frank was coming with us in his baby tent.

We had a big tent, with bedrooms and a kitchen and all sorts of rooms. We had to leave really early and catch a ferry to go to somewhere called White Cliff Bay, where there was a camp we could stay at and all sorts of things for me, Susan, and Sandra to do.

Going on the ferry was exciting, but Mum and Sandra didn't look very well at all. Dad said that they hadn't gotten their sea legs. I told him no, that they had ordinary legs like me.

The Isle of White was a magical place. There were all sorts of places to explore, and you got to the sea by going down a huge great cliff with hundreds of steps down to the bottom. We take our lunch and swimming stuff down in the morning and then come back up in the evening.

I couldn't go swimming, as on the first day after we arrived, I was running round without my shoes on and hit my big toe on a tent peg, and it was badly cut up. Dad had to carry me over to the nurse in the big club house building, and she put a great big bandage on my toe because it wouldn't stop bleeding. Now I can't swim or paddle or do anything. Mum tried to put a plastic bag over it so I could go into the rock pools and look for fish, so it wasn't too bad.

We went exploring all over the island and went into some special place near where a queen lived a long time ago, and I got a seahorse to take home. I also got to choose a tube full of different coloured sands to take home. I think it was called Black Gang Chine and had something to do with smugglers. The No Body who was there walking around said that they weren't smuggling; they had a right to have things, and the king taxed them too much. So if he found something that was wrecked on the shore, it was rightfully his.

He smelt of the sea and had black and broken teeth and scruffy clothes – nothing special just scruffy and dark. He wasn't anything like the pirates and smugglers in the books Mum read to us or on the TV shows. He didn't even look like the pictures in the shop he was walking through.

Mum bought us each a shell full of pebbles that we could eat and a candy dummy.

Chapter 10
The Man on the Motorbike

Time seemed to pass so quickly; no sooner than I had started a year at school, I seem to be ending the same one. Susan had gone from the middle school off into the senior school, and my last few weeks of the middle school loomed.

My whole class went on a field trip to visit the senior school, where we could look round and meet some of the new teachers. We were going to be given a map because the school was so big we'd get lost; this school was the main one in the area, and students from lots of different schools would be visiting on the same day.

Everyone at the senior school seemed to be so grown up. We were to choose the types of lessons we wanted to do over others in the second year there. For now, we'd take set courses, such as English and Maths, but we'd also be given a selection of other things to try to help us determine which to pursue during our second year. I didn't think they'd let me do art for every lesson, so I wasn't looking forward to it.

The classes at the senior school were run very differently from those at the middle school. Instead of staying in one room most of the day for lessons, we would need to move around the school, different rooms being used for different lessons.

The school was made up of a mix of new and old buildings, there didn't seem to be any real control, as children of all ages moved around the school. It was often difficult to tell the students from the teachers, as their ages were so close. You didn't know whether you were walking past a tutor or a member of the upper sixth form.

Another long, long summer – filled with moving house, camping holidays, family weddings, christenings, and parties – was coming to an end. Dad made beautiful wedding and christening cakes, which were lovingly transported to each venue. The tiers of the wedding cakes were carefully balanced on white pillars, one upon another. Dad took care not to damage the crisp piped royal white icing as he assembled the tiers. Dad learnt the skill of cake making and icing from Nan before she got so confused with the dementia. Over the years of our childhood, we girls had all had cakes in every form – beautiful ladies with crinoline piped dresses in all colours, decorated with flowers and diamonds; four-poster beds made with pillars to eat and almond paste blankets piped with icing fit for a princess. When there was a wedding in the family Dad would make big cakes with many layers each standing on four roman pillars one in each corner. The cakes in brilliant white with silver beads, white hand piped flowers nestled on silver leaves with little sprays of white flowers tipped with green. Dad never made two cakes the same.

Before I knew it, it was time to, yet again, go back to school. School was a place that, even after all the years, I dreaded with all my heart; one day, maybe I'd find a place where I fit, with people who didn't judge or think me different.

We had been put into selected classes to match our grade. In my old school, I had a loved maths, liking the challenge of finding the answer. In the new school, I wasn't in the top of the sets but in a middle set. Using the map of the school, I made my way to the science block, one of the older buildings.

Looking forward to the class, I walked into the room; the blackboard was to my left, and a long line of windows was ahead of me. There were rows of science-type benches, along with benches that extended from the windows, which were to be our desks. I felt drawn to sit at one of the benches by the window. I would have to sit to the side of the bench to see the blackboard, but it didn't seem to be a problem to me at the time; it just felt the right place to be.

Along with the others from the class, I sat down, and we waited for the tutor to arrive. The noise in the classroom built, as you would expect when you had thirty teenagers in one confined place. I found myself with more people I didn't know – no one from my old school was there – which put me on my guard. So I sat quietly getting my pens and paper ready then watching, just watching.

As we sat and waited, I took in the colours around everyone; they were so bright – yellows, reds, violets, and whites. Suddenly, my skin began to crawl, an odd sensation, one that I hadn't had before. The sensation grew stronger and stronger and almost gave me an overwhelming feeling that I wanted to run as a man walked into the room; he was tall with silver hair and wore a crumpled tweed suit.

It was the maths teacher, his aura – a word I'd learnt from the No Bodies – who made my skin crawl. The colours of his aura were dull and menacing, like a bad storm cloud. Very few people I'd come across had the type of colours and storms I could see around him.

Sitting in his class, I found that it was better to distract myself by looking out of the window, rather than worrying about the effect he was having on me and the feeling of fear and trepidation he gave me.

It was during these maths lessons, as I looked out the window attempting to distract myself from the tutor's vibrations, that I noticed that the same No Body was always outside the window. He was sitting on a big black and silver motorbike. He had dark wavy hair that was longer than normal, black leather trousers, and a jacket with some sort of picture on the back.

Even though I was sitting right near the window, I wasn't able to make out the words that were below the picture because of the angle of my seat. The No Body's bike made no sound, even though he seemed to move through the air with no difficulty. He was always there when I was in this particular class. After seeing him the first time, I started to notice him both in school and out at other places, as if he was following me. Instead of feeling worried or fearful, he somehow made me feel very safe and secure, as if he was protecting me in some way.

Chapter 11
Negative Vibrations

Within weeks of moving to the new school, I started to realize that the senior school made it very easy for me to vanish. So many students were there that, if I didn't appear at a class, no one seemed to take any notice.

At first, I would often just walk around the corridors. It was during one of my walks that I came to the door of the common room. For some reason, I started to feel a heaviness and chill, which wasn't normal in this area of the school. I took little notice because I often felt differences in the air around buildings. I just continued to walk aimlessly. As I drew level with the open door, a glass flew out with great speed, missing me by the smallest of distance and smashing against the wall into thousands of shards. This was accompanied by the sound of screaming girls and chairs being tipped over.

I automatically stopped, not daring to move a step farther. I asked my spirit friends what was happening. I heard the start of low gruff laughter – a voice I'd never heard before with a menace in its tone that I found alien and scary. The spirit who answered wasn't one I had ever spoken to before. A man's voice, angry and loud, said, 'I didn't ask to be disturbed. How dare you call me!'

I looked around to see if I could see the spirit who had spoken. There in front of me, inside for the first time ever, stood the man with the motorbike. He told me to walk away quickly and not return to the area until he said it was safe for me to do so.

I didn't ask why or question him. I turned and ran as fast as I could down the stairs out into the fresh air, not stopping until I reached the farthest area of the playing fields.

I sat down under the shade of the trees by the ditch, which had originally been a stream many years ago when the area was part of the old farm. Now it was dried up and muddy and blocked by rubbish, debris and leaves fallen from the trees, which hung low over the area.

It seemed like only a few seconds had passed since I'd sat down and caught my breath when the motorbike man silently appeared on his bike. He sat with his arms outstretched on the handlebars, as if ready to ride off within seconds. I asked him many of the questions that were going round and round my head about what had happened, what I had witnessed. He gave me a simple steady reply to each and every question, his voice never wavering, not treating my questions as those of a silly or stupid child.

Quietly, calmly he explained to me that the girls in the common room had been playing with a Ouija Board. The girls thought it would be fun to see if they could 'call up' or 'summon' the dead. He described what a Ouija Board looked like, saying that it was a simple board that had letters and numbers printed and, sometimes, simple words such as 'Yes,' 'No,' 'Hello,' or 'Goodbye' on it.

The man on the motorbike said that Ouija was a very old historic way of establishing basic communication between those who were in spirit with those on the earth. He said that, although it was simple, it was a very powerful tool and needed to be treated with respect and caution when being used and not as a toy or trick.

Ouija could be safely used if certain protections were put in place to prevent negative vibrations or spirits from coming close and using it to upset or frighten those who were trying to get communications. I asked him why I had felt so oppressed as I walked near the room. He explained that, because I was able to have a natural communication with the spirits, I had picked up the vibrations of negativity that were coming from the unprotected board.

I wanted to know why the glass had flown out of the room through the open door, and the man on the motorbike explained that the spirit had built up an uncontrolled amount of energy and that he'd been angry. He'd picked up the glass and thrown it to stop the girls before they went further.

He said that the girls were using Ouija as a joke and hadn't put any protection either on the board or around themselves and they had been tormenting the spirits to come forward. By doing this, they were only attracting and pulling negative spirits forward – spirits who needed to be left alone to work through the lessons about the impact they'd had on people when they were living on the earth.

I'd never come across anything negative about spirit during my life. I asked more and more questions, which the motorbike man continued to patiently answer. I wanted to know what he'd meant about people's impact upon the earth. He explained that, as a person lives on the earth, his or her actions impact those around him or her, not just those in the generation of the person's life but also those in the following generations.

The man explained that, when we return to spirit, we are each given time to review our lives and to see how our actions have impacted others. We can ask questions about our own lives: Did we hurt someone? Did we make people happy? Did we help or hinder others in their lives? We then see how we need to change or develop on our pathway in the spirit world.

He described the realm of spirit, noting that it was divided into different layers; each layer was home to spirits with different types of development needs. Putting it simply, he said that someone who murdered would not be at the same level as someone who cared and protected those who didn't have family to love and protect them.

This seemed to be so simple and right; I understood this within my heart, not just in my head. I asked if that meant that, when someone was using a Ouija Board, only those spirits at the lowest of levels would come forward. The motorbike man explained that that wasn't the case; he said that those from higher realms could come forward if they were asked with respect to come and teach. But most people who used the boards didn't have the knowledge or understanding of simple things such as saying protection prayers, so the boards could be dangerous to use. Telling me he'd given me enough information for now and that it was time for me to return to my school, the motorbike man slowly faded into the air. Leaving me wishing I'd been able to have time to ask about the maths teacher in the school that worried me.

Chapter 12

I Need Quiet, Please!

Over the years, the voices had started to become consistently louder, not letting me sleep. They always called, always talked, making me feel confused, as if I was always under an attack of noise.

The No Bodies wanted to talk to people who were around me – to let them know that they were safe and well, that they were with them and loved them. I didn't want to do this. I didn't want the voices now. I wanted to be normal, the same as everyone else. I wanted to fit in with the few friends I'd made.

But I knew that I *was* normal, that what I saw and felt was normal; the No Bodies had told me that. Uncle Billy said I didn't feel normal because I was growing up. He said I'd become more sensitive to their voices. I told him I wanted them to go away. I didn't want to feel different anymore. I wanted to have quiet.

One day, I went into school, registered, and went straight back out of the building. There stood both the spirit on the bike and Uncle Billy. Uncle Billy called to me, saying that if I followed, he'd show me somewhere I could go and not be bothered by the No Bodies. He added that I would always be protected by my guide, who I'd been seeing more and more of. When I asked him who he was talking about, he pointed to the man on the bike, explaining that he was one of my guides and protectors, who would always keep me safe as I walked on my earthly path of life.

I followed Uncle Billy back into the village and along the long road clear to the other side of the village. We passed all the houses, finally reaching the entrance to the large cemetery; the gates were big and open to allow cars through. Uncle Billy told me that this was the places where the physical bodies that the No Bodies no longer needed were buried. It seemed a bit silly that, when people passed away, we buried the bodies. Why not just throw them away if they didn't work?

Uncle Billy explained that, when people's special friends or family members died and became No Bodies, they missed their loved ones' company; the cemetery gave them a place to go and focus on the loved one who they missed; they would stay and talk to the person, even though he or she wasn't there. He said the one place that the No Bodies didn't stay was the cemetery. They preferred to be at home with their families or in spirit where it was always bright and light.

I found a place to sit and noticed that, for the first time ever, the No Bodies were quiet; I had space to think in my own head. This is when I realised that I had control and a way of telling the No Bodies to leave me alone for a while. Uncle Billy said I had started to grow up in the way

I communicated with my spirit friends, learning how to control them rather than allow them to control my life.

Now, just because I was old enough to be left alone in a cemetery, I had space for me. No one bothered me when I sat there. It was very much like my time fishing, but oh so much quieter.

By the time I was thirteen years old, the quiet times I managed to get became very precious to me. I felt more and more different now, even from my sisters; I even began to wonder if I'd been adopted. My sisters were quiet and well behaved. They always seemed to be doing well at school, and teachers were always expecting me to do as well as my older sister. Sadly, that was something that I knew by then would never happen while I was at school.

My mind had started to feel as if it was in a constant fight. I didn't know whether I was an adult or a child, whether I was talking to the dead or the living. At school, I felt more and more alienated from people my age, and things happened to me that I didn't understand. I was beginning to see spirit with such clarity that it was difficult for me to work out who was earth-based and who was from the realm of spirit.

Travelling by bus and sitting near anyone who had recently lost someone into spirit, walking past an area where there had been an accident in which someone had passed over, passing a site where someone had committed suicide – all these things were beginning to confuse me and make me feel as if I was losing the firm foundations Mum and Dad had given me.

We had moved into a new house, and, although it was closer to the school, the bedroom space was smaller. Susan was sharing a room with Sandra and me. Nan was in the room that was meant to have been a front room downstairs. She wasn't able to manage the stairs any longer and had started to be very confused as to who she was and often didn't know who we were.

The more confused Nan became, the more spirits I saw drawing closer and closer to her. Grandad, Aunty Nancy, Uncle Billy, and many, many others whose names I didn't ask. The spirits talked to her, and she was answered them. But if I asked her about spirit, she didn't understand. She just told me that it was my imagination. Now I felt alienated at home too.

I started to spend as much time as I could away from both school and home. I was looking for answers to questions I couldn't even then formulate. Why was I like this? Why didn't others see and hear what I did? Why did my head spin round and round so fast it made me feel like I was watching the world and time flying in all directions at once?

These were questions even my helpers and spirit guides couldn't help me with. I was trying to run away from who I was – from what I was, really. I sought silence, but I couldn't find it, even in my haven of the graveyard. The mind of a teenager getting confused about the slightest thing was normal; fighting the voices of spirits and those who wanted help added to my feelings of vulnerability.

I tried to fit in with people from school, friends who were in my life for a short time before either they decided to move on or I walked away. I was always the odd one out – in school, with friends, with family, and in life.

Mum and Dad watched the changes in me. They saw their middle daughter trying to fit in with everyone; they saw a happy young lady growing and starting to take the first steps into being an independent young adult. They weren't aware of the confusion I was going through beyond the normal teenage challenges.

I started to be drawn to people from school who were not the same age as myself, often to people who were a lot older. I found that my peers didn't have the same outlook on life as I did. I challenged my family with my desire to wear the fashions of the moment, no more than most teenage girls who had the same demand.

I took a part-time Saturday job to cover the cost of some things I wanted for myself. I first worked at a local supermarket, where I'd shopped since I was a child. The owners had watched me grow from a little girl to a young lady, and now they watched me work in the local chemist. I washed bottles to put tablets in, took the labels off, and got the bottles ready to be put into the steriliser so they could be used again.

Later, I took a job as a junior at a hairdressing salon. I eventually decided I wanted to be apprenticed at the salon. But sadly, I didn't stay at the salon. I moved to another when spirits really began to play and disturb my days.

I hadn't thought about what it would be like to work so closely to other people; I hadn't realised that their loved ones would want to talk to me while I was working. I had hoped that, when I left school and went to work, I would be free from the voices, free from the dead people and the pressure to let people know that there wasn't a death as we called it on earth death truly didn't exist.

Death was just a time of losing the broken overcoat we call a body. I knew that a person's age didn't matter. If it was time to leave a body behind on the earth, if it was time to go, it didn't matter what you did to try to stop yourself or your loved one from dying. If you were meant to go, you went.

School ended, and it was time for me to move forward, to grow up and start becoming the young lady who everyone told me I was growing into.

So many things had happened in my life, and although I was only fifteen, it was time for me to move on. I had a job lined up to be an apprentice hairdresser in a salon in Walton. Much to the upset of Mum and Dad, I had a boyfriend, David Williams, who was ten years older than me. But David seemed happy to accept me for who I was.

Things moved so quickly. My sixteenth birthday loomed, and I didn't yet know that I would leave home within the next few months and decide to settle in an area slightly farther away from my home village and the comfort of my family home.

On the August 13, 1977, I would marry David and would get first one rescue dog called Sandy then a puppy called Lassie. Both dogs would still walk with me for years to come. David and I would divorce in 1983. Then on February 14, 1985, I would marry a lovely man called Keith Germain. But that's a whole different story.

Lightning Source UK Ltd.
Milton Keynes UK
171168UK00001B/14/P